# Understanding
# Retrogrades

## Helen J. Adams

First Edition: 1980
Current Edition: 2008

ISBN-10: 0-86690-056-X
ISBN-13: 978-0-86690-056-0
LCC: 80-51517

Published by:
American Federation of Astrologers, Inc.
6535 S. Rural Road
Tempe, Arizona 85283

www.astrologers.com

Printed in the United States of America

## Dedication

Dedicated to James Garrett
who drew the illustrations for the original manuscript

## Acknowledgements

Appreciation goes to Diane A. Bunger,
teacher and national lecturer, daughter of Helen Adams,
for sharing her knowledge and experience.

Gratitude also goes to students, friends and clients
who willingly assisted in this research and
compilation by revealing and sharing how retrogrades
have affected them.

# Contents

# Illustrations

# Understanding Retrogrades

For far too long retrograde planets have been misunderstood or not understood at all by too many students of astrology. Retrogrades are not really "all bad." For instance, Mercury retrograde tones down outward communication; one with natal Mercury retrograde hesitates and ponders before speaking out. Now, would we not have to admit that in many instances silence is golden? Too bad some of us do not have the opportunity to borrow a retrograde Mercury on occasion.

Mercury retrograde inspires one to recount possessions. In view of bankruptcy records some could do with a dose of miserliness.

Mars retrograde holds rage in check and calms what could be regrettable outbursts. If you have ever been trampled at a bargain sale, you probably wished for retrograde Mars for everyone but yourself.

The geocentric view of the solar system is used by most English-speaking astrologers. Geo is Earth and centric is

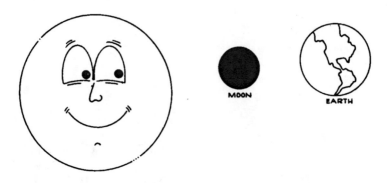

*Fig. 1. New Moon (Sun-Moon Conjunction)*

center; therefore, the solar system is charted as viewed from the center of the Earth.

Neither the Sun nor the Moon is ever retrograde, but it is believed by many astrologers that the Moon is equivalent to a retrograde planet when it is slow in motion, moving fewer than 13 degrees in 24 hours. Most ephemerides give the Moon's daily motion, but it can be calculated by subtracting the place of the Moon GMT on the day of the event or birth from the previous day, if a.m., or from the day following, if a p.m. event or birth.

No attempt is made herein to interpret slow Moons or eclipses, but some simple drawings are included to show more fully the phases of the Moon.

As the Moon revolves between the Earth and the Sun, and both Sun and Moon are in the same zodiacal sign, a New Moon results (Fig. 1). The Moon has no light of its own and only has light it reflects because of the Sun's rays; consequently, in a New Moon formation we do not see the Moon.

The space is so vast that the Sun's rays bypass the Moon to

2

reach Earth; but when there is a direct alignment of the three, an eclipse of the Sun occurs. That is, for a short time the Moon blocks the view of the Sun. It is simpler to illustrate a partial solar eclipse (Fig. 2). By longitude this is also a Sun-Moon conjunction.

An eclipse also forms a parallel. Both Sun and Moon are conjunct within one degree of north or south latitude, interpreted as a conjunction.

The Moon seems as large as the Sun because of the nearness of the Moon to Earth. Not only is the Moon smaller than the Sun but her orbit is shorter than the Earth's path around the Sun. The Moon's orbit is approximately 27.25 days through the 12 signs, while Earth's orbit is 365.25 days around the Sun through the 12 signs.

The Sun's rays reflect from one-half of the Moon, but only a portion of that reflection is in view from Earth (Fig. 3), as seen in the two quarter Moons.

As the Moon, Sun, and Earth are situated with Earth between the two other bodies, a Full Moon is evident, in which case the Sun and Moon are in opposite signs (Fig. 4), or 180 degrees apart.

When the Earth is in a direct line between Sun and Moon, the Sun's rays are blocked out and cannot reach the Moon. The Moon cannot be seen, and thus an eclipse of the Moon occurs. This creates an opposition in longitude and a contra-parallel in declination, interpreted as an opposition (Fig. 5).

As the Moon makes the last lap at the three-quarter point of its orbit about the Earth, the Sun's rays are obvious from half of the Moon opposite to that of the first quarter (Fig. 3).

*Fig. 2. Partial Solar Eclipse*

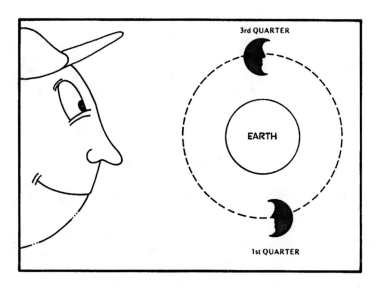

*Fig. 3*

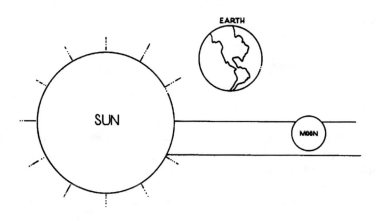

*Fig. 4 Full Moon*

5

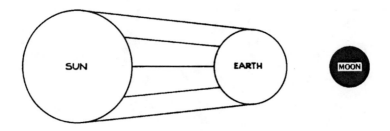

*Fig. 5. Eclipse of the Moon*

The Moon at first quarter and last quarter, or three-quarter position, is in a square or 90-degree angle to the Sun.

Thus a cycle has been completed, making a conjunction, two squares, and an opposition. At some point the Moon made one or more aspects with every planet, cusp, and point in the chart over a period of 27 days and five to eight hours. Meanwhile the Sun has moved less than one sign, with both the Sun and Moon advancing in direct motion since neither is ever retrograde.

Incidentally, the Moon's Nodes always move toward a lower degree; that is, they are perpetually retrograde, spending about 15 months in each sign and completing a zodiacal cycle in approximately 18.5 years.

The planets in order of their distance from the Sun are Mercury, Venus, Earth, Mars, Jupiter, Saturn, Uranus, Neptune, and Pluto.

Note that both Mercury and Venus are nearer the Sun than is Earth. This distance figures importantly in the patterns of retrogrades, and knowledge of the travel patterns helps us to better understand the astrological effect of a retrograde planet (Fig. 6).

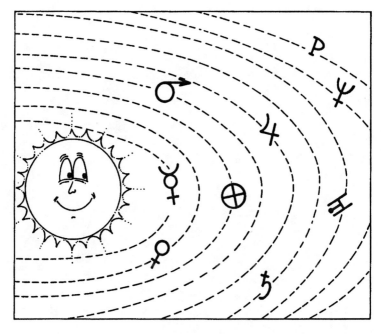

*Fig. 6 Planetary Orbits*

Perhaps the sound of the word retrograde carries with it an element of frightening respect. According to Webster, the adjective is defined as: "1. moving or directed backward. 2. going back to an earlier or worse condition." The verb retrograde means "1. to go, or seem to go, backward. 2. to become worse; decline."

"To seem to go backward" describes retrograde motion of the planets. They only appear to go in reverse direction. Because they are near the Sun and because they travel a path between the Earth's orbit and the Sun, Mercury and Venus are never very far from the Sun. Mercury is never more than 28 degrees from the Sun, and Venus is never more than 48 degrees from the Sun in the chart.

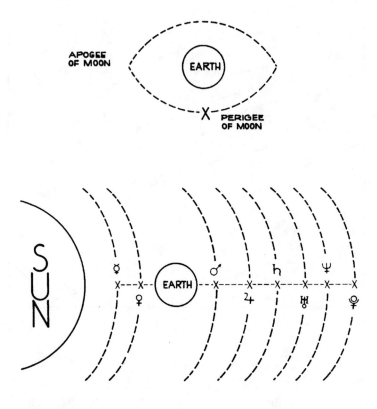

*Fig. 7. Apogee (farthest, slow) and Perigee (nearest, fast)*

A planet is retrograde when it is in perigee, the point in a planet's orbit where it is nearest Earth. Apogee is the point in a planet's orbit where it is at the point most distant from Earth (Fig. 7).

# Mercury
## Retrograde

Mercury is retrograde three or four times each year, at approximately four-month intervals, for a period of 20-24 days. The four-month time variance falls in all or part of the same element each year. Then the variation of days will allow the cycle to shift to another element.

Shown in the sample grid (Figs. 8A and 8B) are Mercury's retrograde periods for 1975, all three of which were in air signs: Aquarius in January, Gemini in May, and Libra in September.

During 1976, the retrogradation occurred in air signs and resumed direct motion in earth signs. All retrograde days were in earth signs in 1977. The complete cycle of retrogrades through all signs is six to seven years.

Note that each third period of retrograde motion occurs near the degree where Mercury had resumed direct motion approximately 10.5 months before. For example, on January 31, 1975, Mercury turned retrograde at 25 Aquarius and direct at 9 Aquarius on February 21, 1975.

Mercury retrograde ephemeris table (R = retrograde, D = direct):

| | ♏ | ♐ | ♑ | ♒ | ♓ | ♈ | ♉ | ♊ | ♋ | ♌ | ♍ | ♎ | ♏ |
|---|---|---|---|---|---|---|---|---|---|---|---|---|---|
| 1973 Mar. 5 | | | | R 28 / D 15 | | | | | | | | | |
| July 7 | | | | | | | | | D 22 | R 3 | | | |
| Oct. 31 | | | | | | | | | | | | | R 26 / D 10 |
| 1974 Feb. 16 | | | | | R 11 / D 27 | | | | | | | | |
| June 18 | | | | | | | | | R 13 / D 4 | | | | |
| Oct. 14 | | | | | | | | | | | | D 24 | |
| 1975 Jan. 31 | | | | R 25 / D 9 | | | | | | | | | |
| May 30 | | | | | | | | R 23 / D 15 | | | | | |
| Sept. 27 | | | | | | | | | | | | R 24 / D 9 | |
| 1976 Jan. 15 | | | D 23 | R 9 | | | | | | | | | |
| May 10 | | | | | | | D 24 | R 3 | | | | | |
| Sept. 9 | | | | | | | | | | | D 23 | R 7 | |
| Dec. 28 | | | R 23 / D 7 | | | | | | | | | | |

*Fig. 8A Mercury retrograde (approximately 21 days, 3 times per year)*

| Date | ♏ | ♎ | ♍ | ♌ | ♋ | ♊ | ♉ | ♈ | ♓ | ♒ | ♑ | ♐ | ♏ |
|---|---|---|---|---|---|---|---|---|---|---|---|---|---|
| 1977 Apr 20 | | | | | | | D 4 / R 14 | | | | | | |
| Aug. 23 | | | D-6 / R 20 | | | | | | | | | | |
| Dec. 12 | | | | | | | | | | | R 7 / D 21 | | |
| 1978 Apr. 2 | | | | | | | | R 26 / D 14 | | | | | |
| Aug. 5 | | | R 3 | D 20 | | | | | | | | | |
| Nov. 26 | | | | | | | | | | | | R 21 / D 5 | |
| 1979 Mar 15 | | | | | | | | | R 8 / D 25 | | | | |
| July 18 | | | | R 14 / D 3 | | | | | | | | | |
| Nov. 10 | | | | | | | | | | | | R 5 / D 19 | |
| 1980 Feb. 26 | | | | | | | | | R 21 / D 7 | | | | |
| June 29 | | | | | R 25 / D 15 | | | | | | | | |
| Oct. 23 | | | | | | | | | | | | R 15 / D 4 | |

*Fig. 8B Mercury retrograde (approximately 21 days, 3 times per year)*

11

On January 15, 1976, Mercury turned retrograde at 9 Aquarius. It turned direct in February 1976 at 23 Capricorn, a near 30-degree offset from the retrograde of January 31, 1975. This pattern repeats, varying only occasionally by a few degrees.

January 31, 1975 ☿ ℞ 25 ♒

February 21, 1975 ☿ D 9 ♒

January 15, 1976 ☿ ℞ 9 ♒

February 4, 1976 ☿ D 23 ♑

Mercury is a neutral planet and may be referred to as "it" because it is both dry and moist. Mercury rules the masculine sign Gemini and the feminine sign Virgo. It is impersonal in nature and behaves harmoniously or inharmoniously, depending upon the planet or planets aspecting it and the signs and houses involved.

Mercury represents the body, soul, and spirit, and combined becomes the ability to think. The soul is a compilation of all the senses. Spirit is energy. The body is the house or dwelling place of the soul and spirit. Mercury then serves as a communicator and is known otherwise as the "Messenger of the Gods."

It is most influential to the health because of its rulership of nerves and also because it could be said the Messenger of the Gods is the link between body and soul.

It is generally thought that Mercury sextile or trine Venus or Jupiter leads to luck and fortune in the natal chart, or if found to form a sextile or trine in transit, only good is expected. Remember that both Venus and Jupiter encourage overindulgence. Such aspects between either of them and

Mercury could prompt one to think (Mercury) he is lucky (Jupiter) and to buy (Venus) more (Jupiter) on credit (Mercury) than he can pay (Venus) for.

One who is overindulgent because of sextiles or trines may be blessed with Mercury aspected by Saturn to lend wisdom to thought or with Mercury retrograde to cause him to consider thoroughly before speaking or entering into a contract.

## Interpreting Mercury Retrograde

Retrograde Mercury in the natal chart will manifest in different ways as to sign, house, and aspect, but there are some basic rules.

1. Consider whether Mercury is leading the Sun; that is, is Mercury in a twelfth house position from the Sun, or is it trailing the Sun in a first house position?

When Mercury leads the Sun in a natal chart (twelfth house position), the native is a quiet, retiring person who completely reviews and weighs all angles before speaking out. He or she is also one who can and will keep a confidence. This is a deep thinker who reviews information to be learned and files knowledge in the mind to be called forth on command.

Mercury retrograde inspires one to redo, review, reread, repeat, rethink, all of which are conducive to learning and retention of knowledge. This is a quiet Gemini application.

Following the Sun, or in first house position to the Sun, there is a shy nervousness which sometimes expresses in halting speech, lisping, difficulty in pronunciation, or stuttering, especially in early life; but which may become very ac-

13

complished in education, knowledge, and oratory expertise by virtue of capitalizing on a handicap. The lack of perfection seems to become a challenge, and Mercury retrograde assists in the rehearsals necessary to eliminate the imperfections.

2. Consider the sign in which Mercury is placed. There may be some irregularities in interpretation because the retrograde motion of Mercury saturnizes the thinking and reasoning process.

To delineate, imagine the traits and qualities of the signs and planets in order to distinguish if they are compatible. A good routine for the planets which rule only one sign is to judge the angle of the sign occupied in respect to the sign the planet rules. A planet located square or opposition its dignity, or home, is not usually as well situated as is a sign sextile or trine its home sign. Mercury and Venus rule two signs each, so the rule here does not work as well there.

3. Consider the effect of the retrograde influence. In various signs the effect may differ.

| *Retrograde Words* | *Negative or Positive* |
| --- | --- |
| Repeat (words) | Does the sign benefit by repetition? |
| Redo (events) | Does the sign accept redoing? |
| Retreat | Does the sign respond to backing away? |
| Reverse | Does the sign perform as expected? |
| Rethink | Does the sign need concentration? |
| Restraint | Does the sign consent to control? |
| Regrets | Does the sign restore easily? |
| Restriction | Does the sign accept limitation? |

14

*Aries*: Aries is impulsive and accident prone. Some rethinking could remove obstacles. Redoing in Aries may uncover previous errors. Aries is impatient, does not like to back up or retreat. It is impulsive and does not appreciate being restrained. This sign is the pioneer that strives for progress rather than reversals. The Aries temperament wants to choose its own friends and partners, so there may be regrets if someone else makes these choices for the Aries individual.

Mercury retrograde in Aries is not usually a fast talker, nor is there a great deal of talk. There is caution in communication. Mercury retrograde in Aries accepts confinement better than Mercury direct in Aries.

If Mercury is in Aries, retrograde or direct, the Sun must be in Pisces, Aries, or Taurus.

*Taurus*: Taurus responds better to the practical ability to analyze as identified with Virgo than to the learning by gathering knowledge as identified with Gemini. Taurus is patient and is not inclined to make careless errors. This sign does not object to doing things over again if there is a reason, but never invites cause to waste time; therefore, repetition up to a reasonable point is valuable to Mercury retrograde in Taurus. Taurus adapts well to rethinking if it is in the form of demonstration rather than reading.

Mercury retrograde in Taurus tends to build up knowledge more slowly, holds on to knowledge and possessions, and then spends both on impulse. This Mercury retrograde talks and communicates more than does Mercury direct and may even go into deep debt, which is generally against the principles of Taurus. Mercury retrograde in Taurus could cause the native to lose patience and be as mad as a bull.

Learning could be extremely slow and negative, or learning could be more thorough and positive, depending upon the entire chart and how the individual responds.

If Mercury is in Taurus, retrograde or direct, the Sun must be in Aries, Taurus, or Gemini.

*Gemini*: Mercury is at home in Gemini and has an insatiable desire to learn. The mind is racing for information at such speed as to just skim the surface of the body of available knowledge. The retrograde causes one to rethink, repeat, and review, thus absorbing more concrete knowledge. Gemini mercurized gathers bits and pieces of intellectual morsels, collecting a brilliant scrap pile and somewhat resembling an unindexed walking encyclopedia. Mercury retrograde then can be a bonus in Gemini in that the retrograde harnesses mental energy and culls some of the unrelated material, such as memorized lists of serial numbers on discarded electrical appliances.

Mercury retrograde in Gemini does not talk unless there is something to be said. Mercury retrograde in Gemini could promote nervousness, especially if the budget gets overspent.

There may be a daily routine of visitation to neighbors and relatives, frequently retracing a well-trod path. Mercury retrograde could return the individual again and again to the same flirtation and may prompt frequent marriage and divorce. There is a tendency to repeat things said and heard at social gatherings—gossip.

If Mercury is in Gemini, the Sun must be in Taurus, Gemini, or Cancer.

*Cancer*: Mercury retrograde in Cancer holds the native in the home, and there is a delay in breaking away from the parents. Psychic talents are evident. Cancer is normally all these things, and Mercury retrograde seems to intensify the natural instincts. Mercury retrograde in Cancer delves into the past and recalls it over and over, continuously returning to the family hearth. It is difficult for Mercury retrograde in Cancer to let go of old, unpleasant memories. Enemies from earliest childhood remain enemies because unpleasant events and unkind words are often relived.

There is constant inquiry concerning childbirth until questions are satisfactorily answered. There is a natural interest in anything related to birth. Any outstanding honor in early life, or honor in the family, will be the theme of many retold tales.

When Mercury is in Cancer the Sun must be in Gemini, Cancer, or Leo.

*Leo*: Mercury retrograde in Leo has a life almost totally dedicated to his or her own children. The conversation centers around the individual's offspring and these people will relate all sorts of events involving their children, as well as going to any expense or inconvenience to provide for them.

Although Leo is the sign of parties and entertainment, people with Mercury retrograde in Leo seek very little entertainment outside the home, including that related to the vocation.

Hobbies are under the rulership of Leo and the fifth house. Mercury retrograde in Leo seldom engages in a hobby. Perhaps the children are the hobby.

Mercury retrograde in Leo is self-employed more often than serving in an employee capacity.

If Mercury is in Leo, the Sun must be in Cancer, Leo, or Virgo.

*Virgo*: Mercury is dignified in Virgo and strives for perfection there. The retrograde motion would thus encourage the individual to unnecessarily rethink, repeat, and review.

Mercury in Virgo automatically analyzes to eliminate all errors, and any repetition is superfluous.

Virgo has already analyzed the hair off of every situation, and any additional analysis is gold-plated nitpicking and can bring on nervous exhaustion. Mercury retrograde in Virgo could rework one right out of a job.

The restraints and restrictions of the retrograde may lead the individual to rethink until opportunities have gone. Mental reviews and redos may well cause insomnia, which could adversely affect the health.

Totally negative use of this retrograde could bring an untidy appearance instead of Virgo's usual neatness.

When Mercury is in Virgo the Sun must be in Leo, Virgo, or Libra.

*Libra*: Mercury retrograde in Libra is in the sign of partnership and justice. There is a tendency to back out on partnerships, perhaps never getting around to marriage, or entangling oneself in several marriages of short duration. Even if the individual remains in a marriage, there is a singleness in the work life. It is difficult to work with other people, and the native often strives to be his or her own boss in a self-owned business, or to work in a managerial capacity with little or no supervision.

Mercury retrograde in Libra is associated with delays in lawsuits and, when possible, the individual should be represented in litigation rather than make his or her own legal decisions; direct dealing would cause delay.

Libra is normally indecisive. Retrograde Mercury rehashes all angles for so long that associates lose patience with the person who takes too much time to decide an issue.

If Mercury is in Libra, retrograde or direct, the Sun must be in Virgo, Libra, or Scorpio.

*Scorpio*: Ordinarily Scorpio is a quiet sign; Mercury in Scorpio thinks much but says little. Mercury retrograde in Scorpio talks a great deal and often issues profound statements.

Mercury retrograde in Scorpio has extensive business ability, perhaps because of Scorpio's determination and desire to gain that which sometimes seems beyond reach. Scorpio is resourceful, and retrograde Mercury increases the ability to skim the surface, similar to Gemini, rather than delving deeply into a subject.

Mercury retrograde in Scorpio has difficulty in sexual expression and has a certain modesty which inhibits conversation on the subject. Mercury direct in Scorpio talks much about sex.

If Mercury is in Scorpio, retrograde or direct, the Sun must be in Libra, Scorpio, or Sagittarius.

*Sagittarius*: Mercury is at its detriment in Sagittarius, which is the sign of the higher mind, or philosophy. Mercury retrograde in Sagittarius converts the mentality into a likeness of Gemini, the opposing sign. Rather than being the professional specialist, retrograde Mercury becomes the knowledge gatherer and evolves as the elementary school teacher or the merchant, which are Gemini professions.

Mercury retrograde in Sagittarius takes on a tinge of the unorthodox in religious beliefs. There is a tendency to rebel against traditional religion, but the creed has been so securely indoctrinated that it never seems to completely let go of the basic religious training. The native has a deep individualistic moral code.

Mercury retrograde in Sagittarius is generous but may want at some later date to reclaim any gift or contribution made. Sagittarius is the big spender, but Mercury retrograde there may prefer to buy on credit, hoping to forget the cost.

If Mercury is in Sagittarius, retrograde or direct, the Sun must be in Scorpio, Sagittarius, or Capricorn.

*Capricorn*: Mercury retrograde in Capricorn relates to the career and to the public. Capricorn prefers to be well-prepared for the job to be done but can proceed on very basic training. Mercury retrograde in Capricorn would lead one to return over and over for more training. Retrograde motion makes it a laborious task for one to make up his or her mind; consequently the career may shift in many directions before the individual settles on a definite source of income. Since handicaps often catapult one to greater heights of accomplishment, it is thus to be expected (Capricorn is the obstacle expert) that Mercury retrograde in Capricorn will seek public appearances often and through many venues.

Capricorn holds an attachment to the traditional, and Mercury retrograde in Capricorn may cause one to hang onto the traditional family career instead of launching out in pursuit of personal goals.

If Mercury is in Capricorn, retrograde or direct, Sun must be in Sagittarius, Capricorn, or Aquarius.

*Aquarius*: You would naturally expect Mercury retrograde in Aquarius to be unique. Research reveals that talking is a prominent part of the career: teaching, selling, radio, TV, etc.

Aquarius is the sign noted for friendship, and Mercury retrograde in Aquarius appeals to large masses. There is difficulty in one-to-one relationships because Aquarius is the sign of returned love, being opposite Leo, the sign of love given. The intuition is keen but unspoken. Psychometry and psychic ability can be developed. Meditation and solitude are important even though they may not be a conscious portion of the daily routine.

When Mercury is in Aquarius, retrograde or direct, the Sun must be in Capricorn, Aquarius, or Pisces.

*Pisces*: Mercury in Pisces is in detriment and is negative and feminine in its placement there. The retrograde motion gives a gift of gab, seeking conversation with any listener and telepathically picking up the attitudes of those in the immediate environment. There is psychic interest and ability, often expressed as psychic healing. There is a strong tendency to "drag one's feet" when in close association with people who are not healthy or who have emotional problems.

Mercury retrograde in Pisces will return repeatedly to the feet of any who give inspiration, and believes explicitly in the personally selected guru.

A weakness for alcohol does not seem to predominate Mercury retrograde in Pisces. Here, the retrograde motion lends the ability to reason positively.

When Mercury is in Pisces, retrograde or direct, the Sun must be in Aquarius, Pisces, or Aries.

## Progressed Mercury Retrograde

Since Mercury remains in retrograde motion approximately three weeks, even one born in the early days of the retrograde period can expect Mercury to progress to direct motion before age 24, using the day for a year method.

In most instances Mercury retrograde in the birth chart will turn direct by progression in childhood or youth; that is, while still under the protection of the parental home. Many people do not remember any event associated with the progressed Mercury turning direct. It could manifest as the ability to speak more distinctly, as increased introversion or extroversion, or as more studiousness or sociability. One could declare a philosophy and request confirmation, baptism, or church membership. For many, Mercury progressing to direct motion marks the time when they realize they cannot read and thus make a dedicated effort to correct this deficiency in their education.

Mercury has an influence on enunciation, use of vocabulary, knowledge and use of the written and spoken language, and the art of learning any of the sciences including mathematics, even in the simplest form.

Mercury rules the hands and reflects positively or negatively in coordination of hands and mental command. A natal retrograde Mercury progressed direct could mark the year someone becomes more dexterous or begins to enjoy making things with the hands.

Mercury retrograde requires the mind to be indecisive; progressed direct, it may cause one to become emphatically decisive.

Those who accept reincarnation believe that what was done in previous lives has to be accounted for in the present lifetime and that debts must be paid. This is supposedly indicated by retrograde planets; theoretically, if and when a planet progresses direct, the debt has been paid. In view of this (be it an absolute fact or merely theory) anyone inclined to accept it can expectantly celebrate the relatively short time Mercury will remain in retrograde effect. However, as noted previously, Mercury retrograde is not necessarily all bad. It could be a diamond to be polished or a pearl to be cultured.

When any natal retrograde planet turns direct by progression, the effect of the influence in the life of the individual reflects accordingly. As seen in the interpretation of Mercury retrograde in the signs, the retrograde factor changes the character of the planet to some extent.

For the benefit of the reader who does not understand "direct by progression," an example follows:

Suppose a child was born August 23, 1978. On that date Mercury was retrograde at 22 Leo. Six days later, on August 29, we find Mercury turned direct at 20 Leo. This means that when the child is six years old he or she will begin to experience the effect of the direct motion of the planet.

For the advanced student, teacher, or counselor who may not have previously taken into consideration the probability of the individual having experienced the full retrograde cycle, let us suppose a birth occurred September 1, 1943. In the eleventh year (1954), Mercury progressed to retrograde. For the following 22 years, until 1973, the individual operated under the influence of a retrograde Mercury.

During the years of retrograde by progression another dynamic impact was undergone by the native. At birth Mercury was direct at 5 Libra. By progression we find Mercury turned retrograde at 9 Libra at age eleven, and continued in Libra until 1967, when it retreated into Virgo. The native was then 25 years of age. The retrograde by progression continued to 24 Virgo, where it turned direct by progression in 1973, at age 33. In 1981, Mercury by progression returned to Libra and continued there for 19 years before entering Scorpio. If the native reaches age 72, Mercury will enter Sagittarius by progression. The native thus would have to adapt to Mercury in four signs during her lifetime: direct in Virgo, Libra, Scorpio, and Sagittarius, and retrograde in Virgo and Libra.

**Interpretation Memos**

When you interpret a natal chart, scan the trail of Mercury from the birth date to the progressed date in order to determine how the thinking, reasoning and learning processes have been challenged since birth, at what stages in life, and how the native dealt with those periods of change. Most likely a progression of retrograde Mercury will return by progression to the degree of the birth chart. This warrants attention because any weakness will intensify and any strength will multiply.

It is wise also to examine whether Mercury is in a first, second, or twelfth position from the sign holding the Sun.

Regardless of house location, even in reading the natal horoscope, the Sun represents a broad passageway, and the planets approaching, existing in, or exiting that passage will behave differently. This is the aura of the ego.

Refer to Mercury retrograde in the signs on previous pages for some vibrations of the natal retrogradation or progressed retrogradation. Consult any reliable text for interpretation of the planet's direct motion.

Once the implications of the planet in a sign have been understood, it is a simple matter to assign house application. Take into consideration that when a planet turns retrograde by progression into a new sign or house it takes a trail from the following sign or house rather than from the preceding sign or house. For instance:

*First House*: Retrograding into the first house means leaving the second house, not the twelfth. The ego then would engage interests in reference to material values rather than emergence from the subconscious as if entering the first house from the twelfth, as when direct. The physical appearance could change because of loss of possessions, or overindulgence during periods of prosperity could bring ill health.

*Second House*: Leaving the third house and entering the second would alter the income or possessions as a result of local travel and contacts, near relatives, contracts or written matters, things of the lower mind and other third house subjects.

*Third House*: Retrograding by progression from the fourth house into the third prompts the lower mind to remember close childhood relatives and may rekindle ties with acquaintances and cousins not seen in many years.

*Fourth House*: Retrograding from the fifth house into the fourth may indicate taking a lover or a child into the home. Since retrograde signifies repetition, it would be someone who had previously been a part of the household or a similar person.

*Fifth House*: Retrograding from the sixth house into the fifth could represent retirement from work or resolution to better health, leaving sickness behind for a life of entertainment and enjoyment.

*Sixth House*: Retrograding from the seventh house into the sixth may bring health problems because of a partnership or may force one to work because of a divorce. On the brighter side it could indicate going to work with a partner.

*Seventh House*: Retrograding from the eighth house into the seventh could mean returning to a partnership because of sexual desires or because of someone's death.

*Eighth House*: Retrograding from the ninth house into the eighth certainly is fitting to religious and spiritual persons. The ninth house represents the training and the ceremony, and the eighth house is the adoration of the spirit.

*Ninth House*: Retrograding from the tenth house into the ninth may represent withdrawing from the career to return to college. Or it may mean leaving public service and returning to a philosophy of earlier life or to a distant place.

*Tenth House*: Retrograding from the eleventh house into the tenth would be leaving the social atmosphere and returning to public life or a career.

*Eleventh House*: Retrograding from the twelfth house into

the eleventh would indicate leaving confinement to return to society.

*Twelfth House*: Retrograding from the first house to the twelfth, in the deepest sense, would be introverting and seeking solitude. It may also mean loss of freedom.

It is approximately three weeks from the time Mercury turns direct until it again turns retrograde. This means that one born shortly after a retrograde period could live approximately 90 years and never have Mercury progress to retrograde; however, no one is exempt from the mischief of Mercury's pranks in the transit of Mercury retrograde.

## Transiting Mercury Retrograde

New students of astrology tend to hide their pens, pencils, and keyboards when Mercury turns retrograde because of all the warnings they have heard about retrograde Mercury.

It is true that there is a tendency to make careless errors and to have the mind play tricks. It is also true that minds made up while Mercury is retrograde often reverse the decision or forget the commitment.

You answer the phone expecting your latest romantic spark, only to discover someone punched the wrong button.

You go to your mailbox and get somebody else's letters because they were mis-slotted. Or letters you sent out the day before are returned because you failed to add a stamp or mis-typed the email address.

A couple of weeks after Mercury goes retrograde you try to balance your checkbook and find you made a mistake or you failed to record an entry.

Completion of actions begun when Mercury is retrograde may be delayed. Related events pop up in subsequent periods of retrogradation and the action usually doesn't culminate until about the fourth subsequent period.

Take advice from experienced researchers: Don't get involved with the Internal Revenue Service when Mercury is retrograde. It takes about five harassing and frightening cycles to clear the most innocent. Mercury is retrograde at some time almost every year during the filing period for income tax returns. Beware!

When you purchase property under the influence of Mercury retrograde, expect the sellers to back out on promises. Be sure everything is completed before closing, or be prepared to accept what you get.

Try to avoid having the foundation of a building staked out or laid when Mercury is retrograde. It is almost sure to be mislocated, and moving a building a couple of feet can be a bit tedious, especially if it is an infringement on your neighbor's property.

A will written while Mercury is retrograde may be rewritten several times before the testator is satisfied with it, or it may never be signed. There are instances in which the will was written and executed smoothly enough, but the testator would have regretted the decisions had he or she known the ultimate outcome.

A will probated while Mercury is retrograde will be difficult to settle. There may be contentious heirs, stocks difficult to convert, complications in real estate transfers, etc.

Mercury retrograde has many advantages. It is a fine time to finish up any project long since fallen by the wayside. It is great for answering correspondence that keeps a friendship going. A book or another work published under Mercury retrograde could bring subsequent reprints.

Mercury retrograde is an excellent time to take refresher courses on any previously studied subject. Recall will be easy, grades will be high, and any new information will be reviewed until it becomes a solid part of the subconscious.

Look for a retrograde Mercury to begin anything you wish to do over and over again, particularly if you can be patient for three-month cycles.

People who sew often find that when they purchase a piece of fabric purchased while Mercury is retrograde stands little chance of being made into the garment for which it was purchased. But how fitting to the reverse motion of the planetary effects it is to change one's mind on a decision. Surely something similar must be true of other purchases.

Just as there are no evil aspects nor any bad signs or planets, neither are there any evil retrogrades. We learn by redoing. We grow in patience when reversals force us to wait. We increase our soul's progress in repetition. The inconvenience of retrograde Mercury may be helpful if dealt with in terms of what we are to learn from it.

Mercury retrograde is not the end of a marriage, nor does it mean the marriage will be of short duration. True, it is a contract of sorts, but marriage or the wedding itself is primarily a ceremony, and the retrograde more accurately implies that there will be something irregular with the ceremony such as repeated vows. Someone may make an error on the license or marriage certificate. There will be a change in the constitution of the marriage when there are aspects to the wedding chart Mercury, or when the retrograde progresses to direct. The wedding chart can be progressed just as any other chart.

Divorces filed while Mercury is retrograde may meet with delay or conflict, or may be contested in court, or the case may be dismissed. Many divorces are filed and granted during the time Mercury is retrograde, but by the time the next cycle of retrogradation comes, the parties have remarried. Very often they remarry each other!

If Mercury is retrograde in a birth chart it may be wise to question the validity of the birth time. Birth registrations certainly are subject to error because they are completed by people. And whoever said the computer is more perfect? It was also made by and is used by people.

## Mercury Retrograde in Health

Nervous tension is likely to occur in the part of the body represented by the sign and house holding Mercury. This may manifest as muscles or organ spasms in that part of the body.

The specified part of the body may act in a manner apparently just the reverse of what one normally expects, or there may be a deficiency in the diet. Virgo is ruled by Mercury, and Mercury governs the functions of the nervous system, with both Virgo and Mercury being important to the bowels.

A physical affliction related to retrograde Mercury will tend to return from time to time.

For general information on retrograde planets in health, see the Retrogrades in Health section.

# Venus
# Retrograde

In any astrological chart Venus is never more than 48 degrees from the Sun. It is approximately 580 days, a little less than 18 months, from one retrograde period to the next, and the term of retrogradation is approximately 40 days. It takes 96 years for a sign to be completed in the retrograde cycle, and more than 200 years for a complete cycle of the zodiac.

A sign may not be inhabited by Venus retrograde for more than 100 years prior to beginning its 96-year cycle, and then it will be in the retrograde pattern every eight years, alternating with two other signs, for the 96 years, until all degrees of the sign have been visited by Venus in reverse motion.

It is suggested that the reader carefully study the Venus retrograde grid (Figs. 9A and 9B) to better understand the retrograde periods. Note that the retrograde occurs when Venus is one sign ahead of the Sun, and that direct motion is resumed when the Sun is one sign ahead of Venus.

Venus is feminine in nature and rules the sense of touch. It is the receiver of both material things and love, and governs

| Date | ♏ | ♎ | ♍ | ♌ | ♋ | ♊ | ♉ | ♈ | ♓ | ♒ | ♑ | ♐ | ♏ |
|---|---|---|---|---|---|---|---|---|---|---|---|---|---|
| 1961 Mar. 20 | | | | | | | | R 29 | ⊙ 29 | | | | |
| May 2 | | | | | | | ⊙ 11 | D 12 | | | | | |
| 1962 Oct. 25 | R 27 | | | | | | | | | | | | ⊙ 1 |
| Dec. 5 | D 12 | | | | | | | | | | | ⊙ 12 | |
| 1964 May 29 | | | | | R 6 | ⊙ 8 | | | | | | | |
| July 11 | | | | | ⊙ 19 | D 20 | | | | | | | |
| 1966 Jan. 7 | | | | | | | | | | R 13 | ⊙ 16 | | |
| Feb. 15 | | | | | | | | | | ⊙ 26 | D 28 | | |
| 1967 Aug. 6 | | | R 13 | ⊙ 13 | | | | | | | | | |
| Sept. 19 | | | ⊙ 25 | D 27 | | | | | | | | | |
| 1969 Mar. 18 | | | | | | | | R 26 | ⊙ 27 | | | | |
| Apr. 29 | | | | | | | ⊙ 8 | D 10 | | | | | |
| 1970 Oct. 20 | R 25 | ⊙ 26 | | | | | | | | | | | |

*Fig. 9A Venus Retrograde (96 years in sign)*

| | ♏ | ♐ | ♑ | ♒ | ♓ | ♈ | ♉ | ♊ | ♋ | ♌ | ♍ | ♎ | ♏ |
|---|---|---|---|---|---|---|---|---|---|---|---|---|---|
| Dec. 2 | D 9 | ☉ 9 | | | | | | | | | | | |
| 1972 May 27 | | | | | | | | ☉ 5 | ℞ 4 | | | | |
| July 10 | | | | | | | | D 18 | ☉ 17 | | | | |
| 1974 Jan. 4 | | | ☉ 13 | ℞ 11 | | | | | | | | | |
| Feb. 14 | | | D 25 | ☉ 24 | | | | | | | | | |
| 1975 Aug. 7 | | | | | | | | | | ☉ 13 | ℞ 11 | | |
| Sept. 18 | | | | | | | | | | D 25 | ☉ 24 | | |
| 1977 Mar. 17 | | | | | ☉ 26 | ℞ 24 | | | | | | | |
| April 28 | | | | | | D 8 | ☉ 7 | | | | | | |
| 1978 Oct. 19 | | | | | | | | | | | | ☉ 25 | ℞ 22 |
| Nov. 29 | D 7 | ☉ 6 | | | | | | | | | | | |
| 1980 May 25 | | | | | | | | ☉ 3 | ℞ 2 | | | | |
| July 7 | | | | | | | | D 16 | ☉ 15 | | | | |

*Fig. 9B Venus Retrograde (96 years in sign)*

kindness, politeness, and musical tone.

Venus is dignified, affectionate and the lover of beautiful things, including jewelry, clothing, and cosmetics. Venus requires comfortable surroundings accented by beauty.

When we find Venus retrograde we can expect some modification in the areas ruled by Venus so far as the interpretation is concerned.

The old symbol for Mars is the circle with a cross at the top. The circle represents the immortal spirit, and the cross represents material matter. Since the cross is elevated, this is a picture of energy directed toward desire for material considerations. The desire is purely physical and based upon sensation.

The symbol for Venus is just the reverse, with the cross at the bottom and the circle at the top. Energy then is the force under the spirit and becomes harmony, beauty, kindness, and love.

When Venus is retrograde, its effect and influence are reversed. This indicates that spirit is energized, causing retrograde Venus to resemble the qualities of Mars. In other words, Venus retrograde can act very much like Mars, which means that having Venus retrograde is almost like having Mars in two places.

The native is much more aggressive, but also has more ability to acquire material possessions, although it will incline toward business reversals for a while. But once the native has learned how to use the energy, the acquisition of possessions has powerful drive and force.

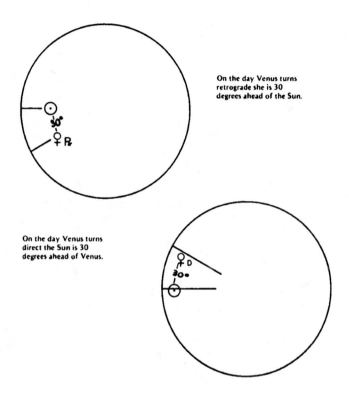

On the day Venus turns retrograde she is 30 degrees ahead of the Sun.

On the day Venus turns direct the Sun is 30 degrees ahead of Venus.

*Fig. 10. Sun-Venus*

Personal relationships are of a different magnitude when Venus is retrograde. The ability to express love is restricted and altered.

Venus is a personal planet and is never more than thirty degrees from the Sun when retrograde (Fig. 10).

## Interpreting Venus Retrograde

As has been previously pointed out, Venus can never be more than 48 degrees from the Sun, and when retrograde not

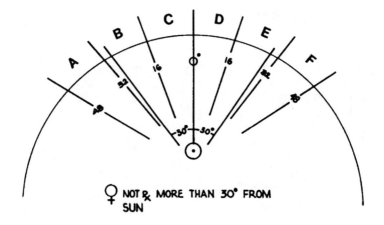

Fig. 11. Interpretation Scale

more than 30 degrees from the Sun. With this limitation it seems important to consider the proximity to the Sun.

For the interpretation we judge according to the distance from Venus to the Sun and whether Venus is leading or following the Sun (Fig. 11).

If Venus is 32-48 degrees from the Sun counterclockwise (A in Fig. 11) the individual seems to have mercurial attitudes toward love and affection and rationalizes whether it is advantageous to form certain affectionate attachments. Much thinking and record-keeping would relate to the finances in some way. Venus would not be retrograde at that distance.

If Venus is 16-32 degrees from the Sun counterclockwise (B in Fig. 11) the individual loves money for money's sake, is an accumulator of personal possessions, receives much in the form of unearned gifts, has a bank account from an early age and maintains a substantial balance. If Venus were retrograde in section B, the Mars-like action would provide energy to attain valuables, but would not have the finesse to receive gifts and would spend at a rate equal to the ability to acquire. The native would be inclined to dive in for sensation and could invest unwisely.

Venus 0-16 degrees from the Sun counterclockwise (C in Fig. 11) would endow one with gentle kindness, politeness, and delicate beauty, having soft, full, shining, possibly wavy hair and probably with full lips and a dimple on the face. Venus retrograde in Fig. 11-C would yield a martian touch of impulsiveness, ruddy complexion, and coarse, unruly hair.

Venus 0-16 degrees from the Sun clockwise (D in Fig. 11) would lead one into secret romances and love affairs, secrets concerning finances, enjoyment of mysterious and occult topics, and a desire to be with few people. Venus retrograde here would reflect a Mars Junior element, which would attract secret enemies and encourage the native to seek enjoyment in darkened places with loud music. There would be no need to be secretive about finances.

Venus 16-32 degrees from the Sun clockwise (E in Fig. 11) would bring secret sorrows, loss of a child or other loved one, or the search for love never being filled. Venus retrograde here does not grieve in silence or solitude but believes that "misery loves company" and shares sorrow, resulting many times in addiction to alcohol or drugs.

Venus 32-48 degrees from the Sun clockwise (F in Fig. 11) is social and intellectual, seeking to share in a benevolent way, and prefers love and affection to be impersonal, such as in friendship. Venus would not be retrograde at that distance.

Venus retrograde takes away the ability to wait in affectionate patience for love to come and replaces it with impatience which may at times appear to be rude or tactless. Love is there but it is like a beautiful piece of art badly displayed.

Material values are governed by Venus, and the retrograde condition brings with it the force to gather an abundance of personal property, money and other assets. There is a natural instinct for accumulating possessions, and yet there seems to be an invisible destiny of loss connected with Venus retrograde. This is not to say that the loss cannot be regained, just that it is a fact to be faced.

**Progressed Venus Retrograde**

Retrogrades carry with them a certain promise that there are lessons to be learned relative to the retrograde planet, whether in the natal chart or by progression sometime later in life. Many people never experience Venus retrograde in their entire lifetime except by transit.

When Venus is direct in the natal chart, then by progression turns retrograde, the interpretation of the progressed retrograde Venus would be the same as the natal retrograde Venus. However, the year of the stationary retrograde progression will be a traumatic one (or several) when material values are lost and love relationships become an emotional issue. The native realizes that love is not being transmitted and received as before. The truth is, he or she has set aside some of the former gentleness and has begun to demand on new terms. The other person does not know what change has taken place on the inner planes of the person with the progressed Venus retrograde and, because of this misunderstanding, accepts the change as a dismissal. Knowing this through advance study of the chart gives an opportunity for better understanding and to alert the other person to the fact that love is no less, it just gets delivered in a different package.

When Venus turns retrograde by progression, divorce may occur.

If the partner's chart also indicates material losses, a mortgage may be foreclosed or property sold at a loss.

Personal property loss may be theft of furniture or money. Investments may reverse and show marked loss, lowering equity value.

Retrograde also means return. Venus retrograde may take one back to a former lover. Remember, there is a lesson still to be learned, but the circumstances will not be the same as they were previously.

Venus is retrograde for approximately 40 days, which in progression represents 40 years. Certainly then one could have direct Venus at birth, Venus retrograde by progression for 40 years, and Venus direct by progression for the remainder of the life. Never would one have Venus retrograde in the natal chart, Venus direct by progression and then retrograde by progression at the end of life. One would have to live more than 500 years for such to occur.

When progressed Venus is retrograde in only the first few years of life, it manifests in such ways as to be denied the opportunity to have playmates, or to be mistreated by brothers or sisters. It may be one who is moved from one town to another so often that he or she is unable to make affectionate ties. It may be a child who is taken out of affluent circumstances and put into a situation of moderate means.

The time Venus turns retrograde by progression in the chart of an older person may mark the death of the partner, or a long-suffered illness of the partner, causing the expression of love to be interrupted.

For one who is dedicated to beauty and who depends upon the physical appearance for life's well-being, retrograde Venus may mean a marring (Marsing) of the physical features of the face.

**Transiting Venus Retrograde**

Love, living, and passions are generally centered in and around the home. Venus is often aspected when there is an event related to the home. (The Moon rules home.) It is inadvisable to purchase real estate when Venus is retrograde, and especially if afflicted by the Moon. One should be most vigilant of the budget and think many times before making investments. Venus is slow to act and more leisurely attuned when retrograde; investments made under retrograde Venus would be a long time returning a profit, if ever.

The period of retrograde Venus marks a heavy schedule in the divorce courts. Venus retrograde is falling out of love and sets the scene for the termination of marriage.

Relate the events of retrograde Venus to the house in which the current retrograde occurs, and also to aspects formed in the chart.

When Venus is retrograde, it is not a good time to start a new source of income.

In interpreting the aspects, you are reminded to interpret retrograde Venus as a Junior Mars.

## Venus Retrograde in Health

Venus rules certain glands, ovaries, kidneys, throat, and veins. Venus is a slow influence, and the diseases of Venus can be expected to be slow in developing and long in duration.

Venus being retrograde in the chart does not seem to indicate any different illness nor better health than Venus direct. Although since retrograde Venus behaves more like a lesser force of Mars, it may well be assumed that any disease attributable to Venus would show its existence sooner than if Venus were direct, and may be accompanied by a slight temperature.

For other information on retrogrades in health read the section entitled Retrogrades in Health.

# Mars
# Retrograde

Mars is the "red" planet, known so because it can be seen with the eye from Earth and appears as a red star. Mars is fourth in distance from the Sun, preceded by Mercury, Venus, and Earth, in that order.

Since Mercury and Venus rotate around the Sun in orbits nearer than that of Earth, they are never very far from the Sun in a horoscope; we see them in the same eye's view from Earth. Mars is the first of the outer planets. Outer planets are those whose orbits are beyond that of Earth. When outer planets at times go "behind" Earth, we cannot look in the same direction from Earth and see both Sun and Mars. This is called an opposition even though Mars is nearer Earth when it is in opposition to the Sun. When Mars is behind Earth in its orbit it is retrograde. This retrograde situation occurs about every two years (Fig. 12).

Earth and Mars travel at almost the same rate; Mars takes 687 days to complete one trip around the Sun, during which time Earth has made almost two trips around the Sun. Only

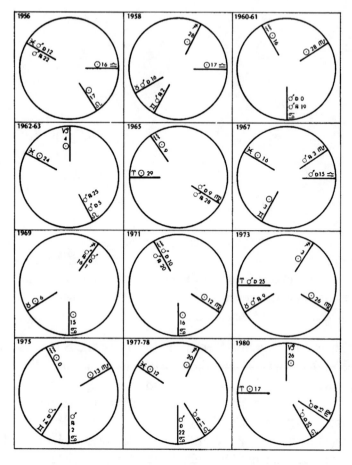

*Fig. 12. Mars Retrograde (79-year cycles)*

one time in the two years do Earth and Mars move into such a position that Mars is retrograde.

The cycle for Mars to retrograde through all of the signs is 79 years. In each episode, at two-year intervals, there is a stationary period when motion almost seems to cease. Ordinarily Mars moves one-half to one full degree per day, but it can remain in the same degree for as long as 23 to 25 days at the turning point to or from retrograde. This extremely slow motion occurs in frequencies of 15-17 years when Earth and Mars are very near on the long side of the orbit. One such occasion was July 1971, when Mars was stationary at 21 Aquarius for a period of 25 days.

Mars may remain in the same degree for as few as five or six days at the turning point. It is this deep burning into the same degree that makes a definite imprint, and of course the longer it is stationary the deeper the imprint.

At some time during the retrograde period Sun and Mars are exactly opposite in the horoscope. The closest aspect of the Sun to a retrograde Mars is a wide trine. Mars remains retrograde from 56 to 82 days, depending upon the arc of the orbit, at which point Earth overtakes Mars.

In calculating this distance between Sun and Mars we find that Mars can fall in the fifth, sixth, seventh, eighth, or ninth sign from the Sun. Of course it could fall in any house in a horoscope calculated for the time of birth.

### Interpreting Mars Retrograde

It was learned earlier that Venus retrograde takes on a Mars Jr. attitude. Then it should be no surprise to find that Mars retrograde takes on a touch of Venus. We would not, however, go so far as to say Venus Jr. The retrograde merely takes some of the sting out of events for a period of time in the life.

John McCormick, in his *Book of Retrogrades,* calls retrograde Mars "the bushwhacker." Mars direct, in most things represented by the position of Mars in the chart, has no fear and strives to fill the desire indicated. Venus, on the other hand, is polite and rather nice about methods of fulfilling desires. Venus is also patient, but explodes when patience finally expires. When we put it all together retrograde fashion, we have a bushwhacker: one who desires but who does not have Mars' bravery; one who tries to appear just peachy to everyone but who snipes from a hidden position. Mars retrograde is not always dangerous to others, but is one who holds back angers and fears.

With this combination of traits in mind we interpret from the position of Mars in relation to the Sun. The first aspect the Sun makes to Mars at the beginning of the retrograde period is an inconjunct, and the first aspect the Sun makes following the close of the retrograde period is a trine. It is almost as if there will be a series of delays and frustrations to be followed by a relaxing but energetic cleanup program.

*Mars Five Signs from the Sun, Wide Trine*: This is the fifth house position and represents children, romance, hobbies, and speculation. The native's attitude in romance is, "All is fair in love and war." Only problem being that love doesn't turn out so good, so soon. It really is a challenge. There are problems in rearing children more often than not because of leniency. Hobbies developed under influence of Mars retrograde may become an avocation for profit after many years of diligent practice and investment.

*Mars Six Signs from the Sun, Inconjunct*: This placement of Mars has a bearing on health. (Read the section, Retrogrades in Health.) It is believed that Mars is energy, and the retrograde influence denies some energy. It is then reasonable to conclude that health problems would arise because the native would not use or exert energy to take proper care of the body, therefore allowing a breeding place for germs. Mars here sometimes leads one into the medical profession.

*Mars Seven Signs from the Sun, Opposition*: This placement relates to partners and spouses, and there no doubt will be more than one. Mars seeks a partner, and the Venus touch supplies it. However, it is a rocky road because this is the bushwhacker, the one who uses partnership for personal advancement. Over the long haul the partner resents being the object of abuse and the battles begin. A marriage can be made to last, but it must be worked at.

*Mars Eight Signs from the Sun, Inconjunct*: This placement is common among surgeons and people in the butchering and meat packing business. It is dealing with death in a kind way and giving life back as a surgeon. The butcher takes one life (the animal) to save another from starvation.

Mars retrograde in the eighth sign placement is not a good place for sex. The native is rejected and, if the remainder of the chart does not protect sufficiently, could turn to perversion.

*Mars Nine Signs from the Sun, Wide Trine*: This position dominates that area related to higher education, and diplomas must be fought for. It is not unusual to operate barely within the law in some way; the individual may be inclined to deny the law in at least one area, such as illegal gambling. It also gives writing and speaking ability for debatable issues. The native holds pent-up irritations concerning religion and philosophy.

### Progressed Mars Retrograde

Mars remains retrograde from 56 to 82 days, which allows for that number of years to encompass the progressed chart.

It is possible to have Mars retrograde at birth and turn direct by progression; and it is also possible to have Mars direct in the birth chart and turn retrograde by progression. It is also possible to have been born just prior to a retrograde period, have Mars turn retrograde by progression, then 56 to 82 years later have it turn direct by progression.

In view of the very slow motion just preceding the retrograde period, Mars will not travel many degrees in the progressed chart. However, only a two-degree orb is allowable in the interpretation of the progressed chart. The progression may indicate Mars changing signs, but Mars will never be retrograde progressed in more than two signs, and usually only in one.

If Mars retrograde in the natal chart turns direct by progression, the native seems to gain courage previously denied in areas represented in the chart by house and sign. The touch of Venus has evaporated, and the drive of Mars becomes explosive.

If Mars is direct in the natal chart and turns retrograde by progression, the native softens and becomes more passive, less aggressive.

In the natal chart the Sun can progress to an opposition, trine, or square to Mars. The Sun is never square, sextile, or conjunct Mars retrograde in the natal chart.

## Transiting Mars Retrograde

When Mars turns retrograde you can expect things to settle down. It is a good time to compromise on discordant issues. All parties will be under the influence of retrograde Mars and will be calmed by the touch of Venus.

But if you love excitement and blood-and-guts crime stories, be sure to get a newspaper on the day Mars turns direct. Mars will be releasing hostilities which have been pent up by the retrograde.

Never marry a person you hope to reform when Mars is retrograde. The direct motion will merely return the same old habits, and there you are caught in the bonds of frustration.

## Mars Retrograde in Health

Mars is important to vitality. The energy flow is interrupted if Mars is retrograde, because Sun in the chart is the ego, and Mars retrograde is in an eclipse position with Earth between Sun and Mars.

For more information on health, see the section entitled Retrogrades in Health.

# Jupiter
# Retrograde

What is the luck aspect? The trine. Wouldn't you know, Jupiter, even in retrograde, would be clothed in jubilance!

Jupiter is retrograde for 120 days, during which the Sun advances 120 degrees, or an exact trine. Meanwhile the retrogradation has been from 10 to 20 degrees, depending upon the arc of the orbit where Earth overtakes the mighty planet.

When Jupiter turns retrograde, it is still within an eight-degree orb (more often three or four degrees), applying to a trine with the Sun. At the end of the retrograde period the first major aspect is a square from Sun to Jupiter, about three weeks after Jupiter turns direct. We have no research to bear it out, but it is suggested that it would be of interest to note what happens at the time of that square. Since a square promises action with results if accepted as a challenge, everyone should get a return from whatever was done during the retrograde period as it relates to retrograde Jupiter and its placement in the chart.

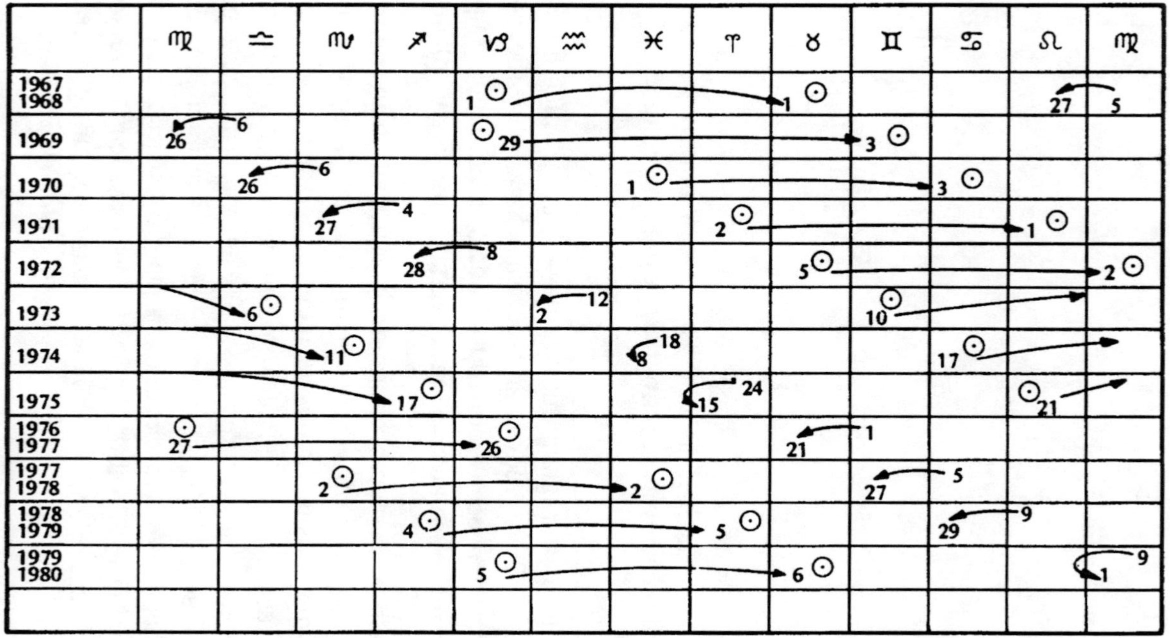

*Fig. 13 Jupiter Retrograde (120-year cycle, retrograde 120 days)*

Jupiter is retrograde every year and makes a retrograde cycle through all of the signs in about 13 years. This cycle, however, is not complete. It would take about 38 years to cover every degree in the zodiac (Fig. 13).

Jupiter has 14 satellites, four of which are in outside orbits and retrograde in motion, moving clockwise and contrary to all other known solar system motion. Could it be that these permanently retrograde satellites set forth a harmony and filter some of the disruptions otherwise possible?

It is said by many that "even retrograde Jupiter is not bad." My contention is, "Whoever thought overindulgence was all good could stand a little saturnizing of Jupiter."

**Interpreting Jupiter Retrograde**

Jupiter in its natural vibrations represents abundance and optimism, giving the native a happy-go-lucky bent toward overindulgence because an abundance of supplies for survival and comfort is always made available by Jupiter. It provides an automatic faith that all will be well in spite of over-participation.

The retrograde condition denies the uncanny luck of Jupiter direct, but affords faith and practicality, endowing an ability to succeed. Jupiter retrograde takes on a degree of Saturn and is not so inclined to freedom. Saturn caution and restrictions seem to cloud optimism.

Just as the symbol for Venus is the reversed symbol for Mars, the symbol for Jupiter is the reversed symbol for Saturn (Fig. 14). Whereas Jupiter is ordinarily much at home in orthodox religion, retrograde Jupiter rebels and alters the moral code to self-made rules. Jupiter is the author of new re-

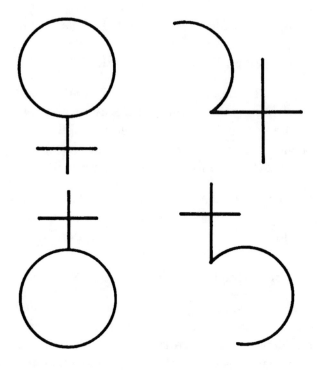

*Fig. 14. Venus/Mars-Jupiter/Saturn*

ligious creeds, and modifies the laws of the land to suit itself.

Jupiter direct is pomp and ceremony; Jupiter retrograde is more modest and appreciative, enjoying and respecting ceremony but satisfied with much less elegance.

Jupiter rules sports, and the native with Jupiter retrograde may be attached to sports as managers, announcers, coaches, or enthusiastic spectators, but may not actually play the game.

Jupiter is judgeship and the legal professions. Jupiter retrograde finds the native associated with an element of the law, but not in the top brackets.

In the natal chart Jupiter retrograde can aspect the Sun as trine, inconjunct, or opposition. The trine may be to the fifth or ninth sign from the Sun, and the inconjunct may be to the sixth or eighth sign from the Sun.

***Jupiter Five Signs from the Sun, Trine***: Romance may not blossom into reality until later in life. Naturally, children also would come later. Since Jupiter is ceremony, Jupiter retrograde sponsors marriage without license in some instances.

Jupiter retrograde in this position should never gamble; it is an assignment to earn, not to win. Jupiter retrograde can be successful in both love and money. It simply requires discipline.

***Jupiter Six Signs from the Sun, Inconjunct***: This position shows conditions of health and service. This is a mark often filled by one second in command. It warrants good working conditions and environment without top honor, but also without burdensome responsibilities.

As the sixth sign also describes the health, one's physical well-being can be expected to be hale and hearty. However, middle age may usher in an undesirable irregularity of the blood. Every instance of low blood sugar known to the author has had this placement of retrograde Jupiter. Cases of high blood sugar have Jupiter direct.

***Jupiter Seven Signs from the Sun, Opposition***: Retrograde Jupiter here falls in the seventh sign of partnerships, and any planet opposing the Sun identifies the native's partners or coworkers. The native will seek a generous, jovial, and moralistic partner, one who has some Saturn traits. The native and the partner will want freedom and independence, but each will be met with unintended restrictions. There will not be the free-wheeling attachment hoped for.

Since Jupiter represents ceremony, and retrograde promotes review or redoing, it is not unlikely that marriage vows will be reviewed or redone.

Jupiter rules honesty. Retrogradation could therefore distort the truth between partners as well as in other areas of the natal chart as represented by the house with retrograde Jupiter.

This is the point at which the eclipse of Jupiter occurs, because here Earth is between Jupiter and Sun.

*Jupiter Eight Signs from the Sun, Inconjunct*: This is the segment representing taxes, insurance, death, inheritance, other people's possessions, sex, and regeneration.

Jupiter in this position may return tax money to the native, but it will also delay any inheritances. Much effort is required to get insurance benefits; strenuous tests may be necessary before policies can be written.

There is some dissatisfaction in the sex life, and although the native has an active sex life, the spiritual quality of sex never satisfies the deepest desires. The native secretly prefers to remain single.

Spiritual beliefs are not totally fulfilling, and there is a spiritual restlessness.

*Jupiter Nine Signs from the Sun, Trine*: The native may have some lessons to learn in getting along with in-laws, but every effort should be made to accomplish this harmony. There will be an interest in laws, if well aspected, and a probable brush with the authorities if afflicted.

Education will be interrupted at the intermediate level, but will be completed later, or education may be completed and not applied to the career. The native may attain qualifications as a teacher, but may emphasize the Saturn quality and organize student activities or promote curricula rather than hold a classroom position.

Jupiter retrograde in this ninth from the Sun position, which is its natural home, often grants success in journalism or publishing.

This is the "modern minister" who leads the congregation in a new creed, keeping the faith but applying the leniencies of the modern day and perhaps advancing a bit.

## Jupiter Retrograde Progressed

Jupiter direct will progress fewer than 20 degrees in 90 years, and Jupiter retrograde is even slower. Jupiter retrograde, whether it turns direct by progression, is direct at birth and then turns retrograde by progression, or is retrograde at birth and throughout the lifetime by progression, seldom moves more than 10 degrees in a 90-year period.

Jupiter turning direct by progression may take one at a mature age into an orthodox church. It would take the doubts out of faith. It may cause one to release the tradition of the family and to comply with personal beliefs in religion.

It may herald a marriage for one who had been a confirmed single, or may legalize a long-term partnership or free one from an incompatible partner.

It may release one from the bind of a long judicial proceedings. Jupiter direct at birth, turning retrograde by progression, will be accompanied by a shattering religious experience and may result in what some call falling from grace.

It may bring problems with law and legal conflict.

It may cause the native to feel restricted because Jupiter loves the wide open spaces.

**Transiting Jupiter Retrograde**

Jupiter is retrograde one-third of the year. The stationary period, whether turning retrograde or direct, is the most pronounced time. The news media will report many stories concerning churches, spiritual leaders, sports events, institutions of higher education, and news from foreign countries.

When Jupiter turns retrograde, any event or project of flamboyance can be expected to slacken or diminish.

It is not advisable to go into a new business venture while Jupiter is retrograde, especially if the new business is under the rulership of Jupiter.

The masses do not spend during the retrograde period as freely as when Jupiter is direct. Consequently, if Jupiter is retrograde prior to the holiday season, shoppers will be more practical, less generous. Those who do buy lavishly will have problems paying for their purchases.

The school year gets off to a slow start when Jupiter retrograde coincides with the opening of the term.

## Jupiter Retrograde in Health

As stated above, Jupiter retrograde relates to irregularities in the blood, and retrograde motion is related to deficiencies in certain blood chemistry.

Jupiter is sufficiency and abundance, but retrograde motion leaves an effect similar to that of Saturn, levying restrictions and limitations on the organs and parts of the body represented by Jupiter.

For additional general information see the section entitled Retrogrades in Health.

# Saturn
# Retrograde

Saturn takes 28 years in its circuit around the Sun. Earth circles the Sun in 365.25 days and passes Saturn once each year. When Saturn is at its point nearest to Earth, Saturn appears to be moving backward as Earth passes by.

Saturn remains retrograde for 140 days, transiting approximately six to eight degrees. However, only about 15 degrees of each sign are visited by retrogradation in a 28-year cycle of Saturn. Saturn remains in each sign a little more than two years (Figs. 15A and 15B).

Within about 10 to 15 days after Saturn turns retrograde it forms a trine with the transiting. At the completion of the retrograde the major aspect is a square.

This is a challenge to honor Saturn, because it delivers as is deserved. Since the opening trine affords an opportunity to act honorably, surely the square at the close will be the hammer on the auction block, the determining factor regarding what is deserved.

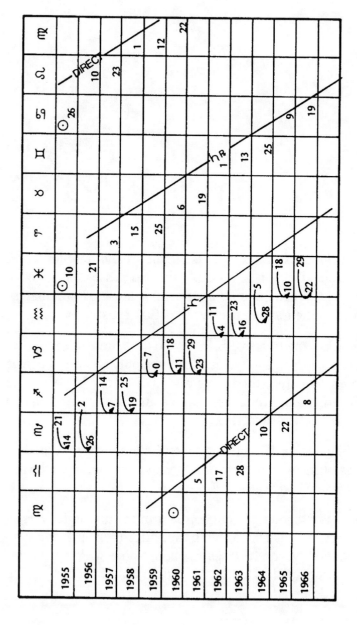

*Fig. 15A Saturn Retrograde (approximately 136 days)*

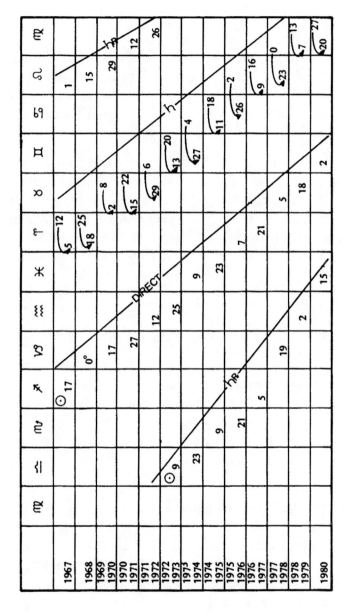

*Fig. 15B Saturn Retrograde (approximately 136 days)*

## Interpreting Saturn Retrograde

Just as Jupiter retrograde is more in the character of Saturn, Saturn retrograde takes on the role of Jupiter. Saturn retrograde in the natal chart gives a flair for extravagance in the area indicated by sign and position. The extreme caution of Saturn is softened. Retrograde is reversing, so the qualities of Saturn are reversed to some degree.

Retrogrades bring with them a background of knowledge or experience as if the native has had previous exposure to whatever is represented by the retrograde planet. Since Saturn is the past, the retrograde makes new things seem familiar. Yet hardships do exist because there are fears often leading to delay in the areas represented by retrograde Saturn.

Some believe that Saturn shows failings in a past lifetime that must be dealt with in this lifetime.

Perhaps some examples would help to illustrate interpretation of Saturn retrograde.

*First House*: Saturn in the first house is almost a sure sign that the father died in the native's early years, but Saturn retrograde in the first shows separation from the father with recurring visits. The parents may be divorced, or the father may work away for long periods of time or may be in an institution.

*Second House*: Saturn in the second is a mark of thrift, indicates sensible, profitable investment results, and is often found in the charts of millionaires. If Saturn is retrograde the native is much more of a spender and finds it practically impossible to accumulate funds because of voluntary spending or undue hardship debts.

***Third House***: One woman with Saturn retrograde in the third had only one brother, and he came into her life only occasionally, always reviving old hurts and usually at the time of the death of a relative.

***Fourth House***: A brother and sister both having Saturn retrograde in the fourth were of a family in which the father was not the authoritative figure but had assumed a more motherly role.

***Fifth House***: One fifth house retrograde Saturn belonged to a woman who was a virgin until she was 32, while another with Saturn retrograde in the fifth was a prostitute. Both were denied love for a long while, then found it abundantly.

***Sixth House***: A sixth house Saturn retrograde accompanies poor health through diet negligence and indulgent habits that promote persistent illnesses.

***Seventh House***: The partner of the retrograde Saturn seventh house becomes a subordinate business partner and functions as an employee. Saturn retrograde, being like Jupiter, indicates an economical business attitude that yields more profit.

***Eighth House***: One record of Saturn retrograde in the eighth is a gay man who is disappointed in his relationships.

***Ninth House***: One person with Saturn retrograde in the ninth has enrolled in college five times. Since Saturn is in Taurus, he finally gave up college for real estate. Experience is descriptive of Saturn, but the retrograde points toward specialized education, taking on tones of Jupiter.

***Tenth House***: Saturn direct is stable and of long duration, but Saturn retrograde in the tenth house keeps the native going from one job to another because of tough breaks. These people think they know the business better than their employer, which indeed they sometimes may. The retrograde holds back adequate compensation, and honor is denied; consequently the native moves on to another position, hoping to be luckier next time.

*Eleventh House*: Saturn retrograde in the eleventh keeps in contact with friends. High goals are set and almost reached, then set aside for some reason. One woman is a club joiner but participates only a little. Another woman feels a need to be punished by her lover; the eleventh is the house of returned love.

*Twelfth House*: Saturn retrograde in the twelfth takes one into confinement through deception, pretended illness, taking the rap for someone else, or by making excuses for not attending a social function.

For further interpretation we can look at the aspects between Saturn and the Sun.

The first possible major aspect, from the beginning of the retrograde period, is a trine to Saturn, then an inconjunct, followed by the opposition, then another inconjunct, and finally a closing trine.

Saturn is retrograde approximately 136 days each year, and the retrograde station occurs about 135 degrees from the Sun in an aspect called a sesquiquadrate. This aspect is said to behave like Saturn. Thus the stage is set for a challenge.

The first major retrograde aspect to the Sun is a trine

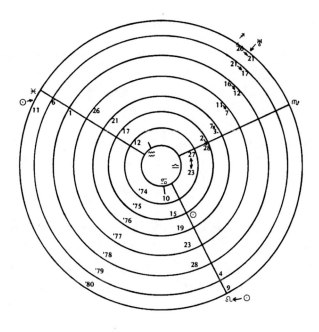

*Fig. 16 Retrograde Midpoints*

with Saturn, which would be nine signs from the Sun. This is a training zone where one is prepared for performance.

The next major aspect the Sun makes to retrograde Saturn is an inconjunct, with Saturn eight signs from the Sun; this is a time for reformation.

At midpoint to the degree of retrograde and direct, the Sun is exactly opposite Saturn (Fig. 16). This is a time of serious awareness.

The next aspect is another inconjunct, with Saturn six signs from the Sun. It is a time to inventory and reorganize in readiness for the last trine at the close of the retrograde period, after which is the square, waiting to produce action.

## Progressed Saturn Retrograde

When the natal chart is progressed and Saturn turns retrograde by progression, the progressed Sun first makes a trine with Saturn, followed by an inconjunct 30 years later, and then an opposition 30 years after that.

This person will have the Saturn retrograde influence in education, religion, eighth house matters, and physical exercise.

When Saturn in the birth chart is retrograde and progresses to direct, it is at the close of the retrograde period and will encompass the last phases and aspects to the progressed Sun. This native will experience a Saturn retrograde influence on children, romance, and service and, depending upon the age and life span, may have a square from progressed Sun to Saturn.

Because Saturn remains retrograde for approximately 136 days, one born in the early period will not live long enough for Saturn to progress direct.

## Transiting Saturn Retrograde

Saturn rules business, careers, and the public. It is not wise to go into a new career or business, or to launch a campaign for anything that depends upon public appeal, while Saturn is retrograde.

Transiting retrograde Saturn in aspect to Saturn in the birth chart could be of importance. Since retrograde calls for redoing, if there are good aspects to natal Saturn, the retrograde may help to revive an endeavor.

## Saturn Retrograde in Health

Saturn rules diseases of long duration, and retrograde motion seems to speed up the process, changing to a more Jupiter-like action. The native is more carefree and negligent of health matters.

Illnesses are caused by some kind of sadness, either confessed or unconfessed, and it may be an attitude or burden the native does not consciously recognize. But the inner body knows of the disharmony and responds by restricting proper functions of the body in the area indicated by Saturn retrograde and the sign in which it is found.

# Uranus
# Retrograde

Uranus spends seven years in a sign, 84 years in a full cycle around the Sun, and is retrograde over a span of four to five degrees each year as Earth reaches the point nearest to Uranus; that is, when Uranus and Earth are on the same side of their orbits around the Sun. On the day of nearest contact, Earth is in a position to eclipse Uranus from the Sun.

Uranus remains retrograde for a period of 148 days, the approximate number of degrees of an inconjunct. Uranus is the unexpected and the instigator of events out of the native's control. The inconjunct aspect also is a bit out of control and is a part of a configuration called the Yod or Finger of God.

The first aspect the Sun makes to Uranus at the beginning of the retrograde period is a trine, then an inconjunct, an opposition, a second inconjunct, and finally a last trine before Uranus turns direct.

For the retrograde pattern of Uranus see Fig. 17.

71

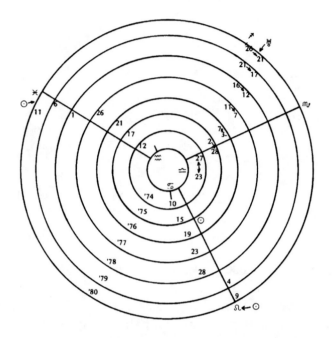

*Fig. 17 Uranus Retrograde (148 days)*

## Interpreting Uranus Retrograde

This is the rabble-rouser. Raising Cain for a cause is important to the native. Uranus direct seeks freedom for self and for personal identity and independence; but Uranus retrograde defends the course of others, especially in the field of medicine and religion.

***Uranus Five Signs from the Sun, Trine***: Uranus is inventive but not at all practical. Uranus retrograde in the fifth sign from the Sun gives the creative ability to use things from the past and to make something useful.

The retrograde cuts down on the unexpected element of Uranus, but there are problems in child bearing and promotion of creative projects. Mental capability is evident, but delays must be met.

*Uranus Six Signs from the Sun, Inconjunct*: This position of Uranus retrograde requires one to create a job, to be self-employed, or to become attached to someone who will be supportive.

This is a predisposition for an appendectomy because the sixth house rules the intestines and health. Illnesses are sudden, and the native heals rather rapidly. These people heave the ability to heal themselves more completely than does a physician, probably because they are aware of what they did to cause the illness.

Many physicians, diagnosticians, and specialized nurses have this position of Uranus retrograde.

*Uranus Seven Signs from the Sun, Opposition*: This native marries suddenly, more than once, and marriages end suddenly, but not always in divorce. This placement is not good for business partnerships.

*Uranus Eight Signs from the Sun, Inconjunct*: The native has problems in sexual expression of love. An unusual event can delay an inheritance, and taxes and insurance demand frequent attention. The native is subject to serious accidents. Many surgeons have this placement of Uranus retrograde.

*Uranus Nine Signs from the Sun, Trine*: The native experiences ESP and dreams intuitively. Vocational training is interrupted, and the native becomes self-educated. The spiritual life is within the creation of the self, and there is a certain inharmony with orthodox religion.

## Progressed Uranus Retrograde

There is much change in the life of the individual during the years encompassing Uranus' change in direction, whether to retrograde or to direct. Uranus progressing direct dictates more freedom for the native; Uranus progressing retrograde gives energy on demand or in defense of a cause for general principles or for universal benefit.

In the area where one felt freedom under direct Uranus, the retrograde may bring imprisonment. Where there is restriction under a natal retrograde Uranus, direct motion may bring freedom.

Uranus also represents tolerance, and its change of direction affects the native's views of others. Direct motion indicates liberal tolerance, while retrograde motion is critical and levies limitations on others.

## Transiting Uranus Retrograde

Watch the days near a change of direction for news reports on unusual events. The sudden and unexpected will occur, and these events will draw people together in common interest and friendship.

Accidents occur under Mercury retrograde, and accidents occur under Uranus aspects. Uranus accidents are peculiar and sudden.

## Uranus Retrograde in Health

Uranus vibrates on a higher octave of Mercury. Its influence relates to the intuitive mind and mental creativity. Uranus and the Moon are the primary instigators of change, especially sudden change. Moon changes are the result of emotional action and Uranus change sweeps away the old to make way for a free future.

Uranus is prominent in astrological interpretations of light and light rays. This means that eyesight is in some way connected with Uranus. An instance of this is that when going from light to darkness or from darkness to light a time of eye adjustment is required. This being so, then Uranus has some influence on sunshine, which in health would relate to sunbathing, ultraviolet light, X-rays, or electrical treatments such as shock treatments used to treat mental illness.

Any illness related to Uranus in the natal chart is likely to manifest suddenly, whether Uranus is direct or retrograde. Transiting Uranus direct may bring the unusual, or the first of its kind in the community, and it may last until transiting Uranus goes retrograde, allowing dispensation of the disease. Illness contracted while Uranus is retrograde may indicate an old ailment resurfacing.

People who have Uranus retrograde in the natal chart seem to know intuitively what their bodies need or what the deficiency might be even when a physician is uncertain. This can prompt the individual to resort to unique procedures for self-healing.

# Neptune Retrograde

Neptune remains retrograde for 150 days, two days longer than Uranus. The pattern of the Sun to the retrograde station is very similar to that of Saturn, Uranus, and Pluto (Fig. 18).

Neptune spends about 14 years in a sign and 165 years in a complete cycle of the zodiac. Considering that Neptune is retrograde almost half the year, we can estimate that more than half the people will have a direct Neptune in the chart. On the other hand, since Neptune is retrograde for 150 days, we can also assume that 41 percent of the people have Neptune retrograde in the natal chart.

## Interpreting Neptune Retrograde

In direct motion Neptune represents deception, idealism, romanticism, and a talent for art and music. Deception is not facing facts, and suffering in secret. A kinder and in many instances a more accurate word for deception is illusion. This is the artistic connotation of Neptune

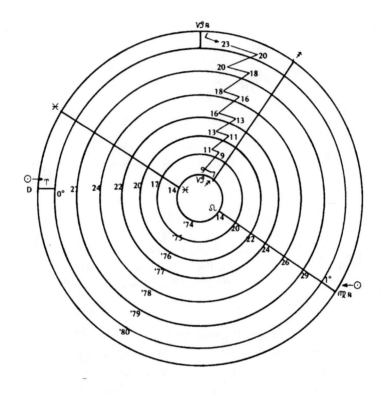

*Fig. 18. Neptune Retrograde (150 days)*

which influences photography, film, and illusory matters.

Neptune becomes more realistic and less secretive when retrograde. The photographer with Neptune retrograde photographs real situations, catching people in natural circumstances, while Neptune direct deludes with fantasy in photography.

Neptune direct prays with the most sincere faith that the

request will be granted, while Neptune retrograde prays and "pussy foots" to the prayers by helping things along, doing something about the request. Sometimes Neptune retrograde is like the woman who prayed for the mountain to be removed from blocking her view of the world. When she arose from her knees, she went to the window, only to find the mountain was still there. She fussed, "Just as I thought, if you want anything done you have to do it yourself."

John McCormick calls Neptune retrograde "open heartedness." This gives Neptune retrograde a generous attitude along with a more practical approach.

During the retrograde period the major aspects of the Sun to Neptune are trine, inconjunct, opposition, another inconjunct, and a final trine, occurring in the fifth, sixth, seventh, eighth, and ninth signs from the Sun.

An event or birth occurring in the very latest degrees of the retrograde period may show Neptune retrograde four signs from the Sun; however, this does not occur as frequently as the other placements.

The fourth sign from the Sun relates to the home, parents, and private life. This is not a square aspect and is not to be interpreted as such; it simply amounts to an equivalency of Neptune retrograde in the fourth house.

***Neptune in the Fourth Sign from the Sun***: Neptune direct would take the native to the seashore, but Neptune retrograde seeks waterfalls and streams in the mountains. It is one who enjoys being in the dark in the home. This position seeks and must have privacy when at home. It also indicates one who takes part in public activities and reaches great heights in a career though working behind the scenes.

***Neptune in the Fifth Sign from the Sun, Trine***: This placement endows the native with dramatic showmanship. This is the natural place for the Sun, so Neptune here gives a double ego, and faith in self is multiplied. The fifth sign from the Sun influences hobbies and talents.

***Neptune in the Sixth Sign from the Sun, Inconjunct***: Compassion is extracted from Neptune when it is retrograde, and the sixth sign from the Sun is service for compensation or reciprocal service, not a service of love.

***Neptune in the Seventh Sign from the Sun, Opposition***: Neptune direct in the seventh house gives an unfaithful or deceptive partner unless it is one of great idealism (spiritual or religious). Neptune retrograde supplies a partner who is loyal and supportive behind the scenes.

***Neptune in the Eighth Sign from the Sun, Inconjunct***: Neptune in the eighth sign from the Sun seeks idealism and romanticism in sex. The person with Neptune retrograde in the eighth sign from the Sun can love without sex and still remain devoted. This planet in this position denies inheritance, but Neptune retrograde in this position grants financial sharing with the partner.

***Neptune in the Ninth Sign from the Sun, Trine***: The native is a philosopher, whether in religion, sports, or politics, and has a strong influence on the public. This is the twelfth position to the tenth of the public, and Neptune retrograde here seems to stimulate and excite people.

## Progressed Neptune Retrograde

The native with a retrograde Neptune that progresses to direct will become more vague in the area of life influenced by Neptune in the chart. Where there had been open-heartedness, romanticism will enter, and an attitude of spiritual faith may seem fanatical to others.

The native with a direct Neptune that progresses retrograde will be the one who sets aside deception in love, or the gambler who faces the fact of potential loss.

If the birth is at the early stage of the retrograde period, Neptune will not progress direct in a lifetime. Nor will Neptune progress retrograde if the birth occurred in the early days of direct motion.

## Transiting Neptune Retrograde

Neptune remains retrograde 150 days, or two-fifths of a year. During the months that Neptune is direct the public as a whole responds to Neptune's traits of idealism, illusion, and romanticism. During the months that Neptune is retrograde the general public responds to Neptune's reverse traits, and there is more open-heartedness and realism.

During the 150 days that Neptune is retrograde, there is little or no room in the zodiacal pattern for dishonesty. Consequently, strange facts will surface.

## Neptune Retrograde in Health

Neptune represents inspiration and may take the form of vapor, color, vision, or pretense. In illness the disease may be one developed in sympathy toward someone else. where the native will experience the pain of a loved one's disease. Neptune is prominent in communicable diseases when the source of contact is mysterious. Neptune may bring deferred pain to the body in one organ or muscle when in fact a different part of the body is afflicted.

Neptune direct seeks a pain-killer in one form or another, whether medical, narcotic or by mental blocking. Neptune retrograde prefers not to acknowledge the existence of the need for health correction.

Perhaps the key word for Neptune, whether direct or retrograde, is trickery. The mind, either consciously or unconsciously, refuses the straight line of fact concerning not only discomforts but the symptoms related to Neptune illnesses. Neptune is not always afflicted when it is the health indicator. Remember: when Neptune is trine the Sun, Neptune is retrograde.

# Pluto
# Retrograde

Tiny Pluto is situated so far out in the solar system that Uranus had to grant the ability to invent a more powerful telescope, and Neptune had to inspire the search, before it could be found.

Pluto is power, deep volcanic power. It gathers followers until it touches the masses. The desire within contemplates until it has gathered strength, and then propels outward with the thrust of a rocket.

Pluto is retrograde approximately 150 days each year.

Both astrologers and astronomers know that Pluto's orbit is strange and they have no positive answer as to why the gravitational pull is so far off center in the ecliptic.

Although Pluto now stays only a few years in each sign compared to 100 years ago, the retrograde pattern is approximately the same; but the degrees were tighter in the past because of its long transits (Figs. 19 and 20).

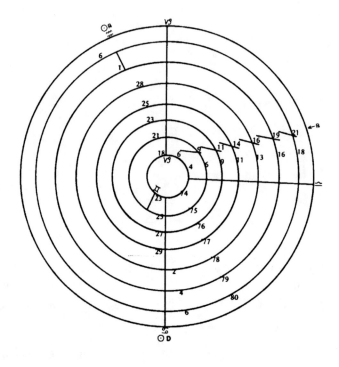

*Fig. 19 Pluto Retrograde*

## Interpreting Pluto Retrograde

Pluto gives power to any planet it aspects, none stronger than Pluto conjunct the Sun. As is true in the case of Jupiter, Saturn, Uranus, and Neptune, Pluto is never retrograde when conjunct the Sun, but always retrograde when opposite the Sun.

Pluto direct is power; Pluto retrograde is dependency. Pluto direct is the leader of the masses; Pluto retrograde follows the masses.

Pluto is muscles, and Pluto retrograde often inspires the

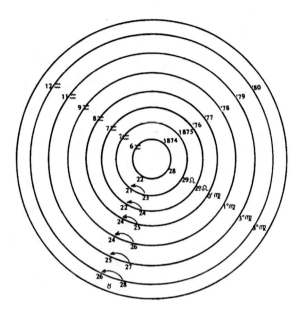

*Fig. 20 Pluto Retrograde*

building of muscles to capitalize on a handicap. There is inner strength.

Pluto direct shows where there is great change. Pluto retrograde refuses to change self, but does endeavor to change others.

It has been established that people with Pluto retrograde, regardless of position, have much inner strength for recuperating from illness. Pluto retrograde opposite the Sun is often in the chart of one who loses the partner in death and who never makes another strong attachment. Sexual desire dies with the partner in many instances.

Rather than promoting inward change to be projected outward, Pluto retrograde represents an immovable force in that area of the chart holding Pluto.

Pluto is the ruler of Scorpio, and it thus seems that the dynamic sexual expression of Pluto is either perversion, or inactivity, the two extremes of normal sex.

Pluto retrograde is a brave leader of the masses, for the masses, not a leader to be an egotistical dictator, as in Pluto direct.

## Pluto Retrograde Progressed

There will be a strong and definite change in the individual if progressed Pluto changes direction, and very powerful forces are felt when other planets progress to aspect the natal Pluto.

Pluto is the reawakener. A change in Pluto's direction will bring a change in attitude toward things relating to the dead and toward spiritual beliefs. Pluto rules the mysteries of life and the spirit world, both good and evil. Therefore, attitudes in occult sciences will change. All religions fall into the occult category if they in any way involve a belief in spirits which transform the person.

The change in direction of progressed Pluto could lead one into an entirely different kind of life.

## Transiting Pluto Retrograde

Pluto is the slowest of planets in motion and sometimes will stay several months in the same degree. The vibrations are extremely forceful when Pluto transits to conjunct another planet in the natal chart.

The orb of aspect from Pluto should be no more than two degrees.

When Pluto changes direction, news stories focus on death, taxes, and sexual assaults. Not all Pluto-related events are negative, however. The news may also include the capture of notorious criminals. Kidnaping is under the rulership of Pluto, and a kidnaping or murder case may be solved when Pluto is retrograde.

Pluto is research, and aspects to transiting Pluto may trigger cures for diseases that were formerly fatal. This is a positive form of Pluto, when life-sustaining science is made successful.

## Pluto Retrograde in Health

Several years ago Diane Bunger was making a study of prominent athletes and found a great predominance of them to have Pluto retrograde. It was also evident by going back to the beginning of their athletic careers that many of them had gained unbelievable strength of body and muscles after having had a childhood disease which could have left permanent damage.

Pluto retrograde gives inner strength to regenerate the various weakened parts of the body. Pluto is spiritual power. In direct motion this power is projected outwardly, but retrograde motion projects the power inwardly.

When Pluto is the implicator or is prominent in an illness it is very difficult to diagnose the disease and the dates Pluto changes direction will indicate a change in the illness, either through the treatment or medication or through the inner healing. Pluto is often the implicator when surgery is involved because Pluto represents removal and surgery. It would also be the death of the removed organ.

# Additional
# Observations

Retrogrades are found in the charts of those who overcome handicaps to achieve greatness.

Retrograde planets should be noted in terms of whether aspects are applying or separating.

Sun is the ego, and the retrogradation of Mars, Jupiter, Saturn, Uranus, Neptune, and Pluto at the peak is an alignment of Sun, Earth, and planet. Each planet can form an eclipse with the Sun, in the same format as a Full Moon; that is to say, the Sun is opposite the planet. The ego (Sun) then is in full face of awareness to the planet.

Any outer planet (Jupiter, Saturn, Uranus, Neptune, Pluto) exactly opposite the Sun is retrograde. The planet is at midpoint between the degree it turned retrograde and the degree it will turn direct. Also the Sun is at midpoint between the degree it was on the day the planet turned retrograde and the degree it will be on the day it will turn direct. See example of Saturn in Fig. 16.

When Mars is trine the Sun, it is always direct.

When Jupiter is trine the Sun, it is stationary or retrograde.

When Saturn, Uranus, Neptune and Pluto are trine the Sun, they are always retrograde.

Mars, Jupiter, Saturn, Uranus, Neptune, and Pluto, retrograde in the fifth to seventh sign from the Sun, are in the closing of the retrograde period and may progress direct. Those same planets in the seventh to ninth signs from the Sun are in the beginning of the retrograde period, and it is doubtful that they will progress direct in a lifetime.

People of prominence and success tend to attain notoriety in fields under the rulership of their native retrograde planets, especially if located in a house related to or aspecting a kindred zone of interest. Some examples are:

Stephen Collins Foster, music, Neptune retrograde

J. P. Morgan, finance, Saturn retrograde

Albert Einstein, math, Uranus retrograde

Mark Twain, writer, Jupiter retrograde

Walt Disney, film and fantasy, Neptune retrograde

J. Edgar Hoover, law enforcement, Jupiter retrograde

When a planet turns direct by progression, the native should feel released from something. The debt is paid.

When a planet turns retrograde in transit, it offers an opportunity to finish up something that has been started. It may provide a cleaning-up and sweeping-away of debris from the past.

To wait to do something until all retrogrades are past

would be impractical and unwise. The pattern of aspects the Sun forms to retrograde outer planets is constructive. The aspects of the Sun to retrograde Saturn, Uranus, Neptune, and Pluto are two trines, two inconjuncts, and an opposition.

Some believe that a retrograde is always bad and a trine is always good; or unfavorable and favorable. When the trines that occur between the outer planets and the Sun are investigated, we find that even Jupiter is trine and retrograde. You be the judge. Is a trine unfavorable when the planet is retrograde, or is a retrograde favorable because it is trine? Interpret that Jupiter as a Saturn trine, and you will get something which comes in time, with work.

## Aspects of Retrograde Planets

There is no mathematical difference in the calculation of aspects to retrograde planets, but it does need to be noted that the motion will change the direction of the planet in terms of its separating or applying. When planets or aspects are applying, they are drawing closer together; when they are separating they are moving apart.

A planet retrograde at 23 Cancer is applying in aspect to planets in earlier degree of other signs, but is separating from planets in later degrees of other signs.

When a retrograde planet is in aspect to another planet, the interpretation must include the retrograde. If the retrograde planet is aspecting a conjunction of two or more planets, the aspect of each planet to the retrograde planet must also be expressed. Note which aspect is first to culminate: it will govern the first events. Other events will follow according to the other planets in order of their placement.

## Retrogrades in Health

Very little information is available on the effect of a retrograde planet on health. It has been written that persons with several retrograde planets in the natal chart suffer a restlessness and undergo hardships due to (some say) karma and having to return to redo something that was not done morally or correctly in a former life. The subconscious assignment seems to dictate burdens.

It is an accepted fact that health is more nearly perfect without stress, and many retrograde planets may add undue stress which may be harmful to the health. Retrograde planets seem in most instances to delay illness.

When a planet turns retrograde, a disease connected to that planet will become disorganized, and the disease's progress will be temporarily interrupted while the planet is retrograde in that sign.

It has also been found that when a planet is stationary the disease is in a state of dissolution. This indicates that the contributing factors of the planet, whether they are of a positive or negative nature, are brought to a standstill, allowing the negative force of the planet to operate. This indicates that if a positive, or remedial, force could be administered to the patient, the disease should be subject to elimination.

Retrograde planets imply that there is a deficiency of elements ruled by the planet and deterioration to the part of the body indicated by the sign and planet in which the retrograde occurs.

See *Encyclopedia of Medical Astrology* by H. L. Cornell for more specific details on particular diseases.

## House Cusps

It has been found that a house ruled by a retrograde planet also reflects the retrograde. For example:

A woman who has Neptune retrograde in the fifth house, with Neptune ruling the second, says that anything she does of an artistic nature must have a function other than to merely be there. It must serve a purpose and possess a value.

A man with Neptune retrograde in the first house takes photographs of realistic things and people in the natural state. Neptune rules the tenth, and photography is not and never has been a business for him.

It has also been found that if a retrograde planet is interpreted as if it were in the opposite house, it renders accurate meaning. If the retrograde planet is in Leo, interpret it as being in Aquarius. If the retrograde planet is in Gemini, interpret it as being in Sagittarius. Change only the house cusp of the house with the retrograde planet; all others remain the same, including the opposite sign (house).

94

Printed in the United States
115644LV00002B/115-162/P